The Even Years of Marriage

The Even Years of Marriage

poems

Ash Bowen

Dream Horse Press
Aptos, California

Dream Horse Press
Post Office Box 2080, Aptos, California 95001-2080

Printed in the United States of America
Published in 2013 by Dream Horse Press

ISBN 978-1-935716-30-3

Cover artwork:

American Couple #1
by Geoffrey Greene

www.geoffreygreene.com

To my loves—Annabeth and Max

CONTENTS

ONE

Based on a True Story   11
Watching an Esther Williams Film after My Wife's Affair   12
The Crossing   13
Sterile   14
To the Double Helix   15
Stork   16
Ultrasound   17
Wolf   18
There Was No Funeral   19
Mexico's Waters Are Only for Newlyweds   20
The Last Known Love Letter of Poseidon   21
Using the Earth as a Blunt-Force Object   22
All My Grudges I've Given Your Name   23
Twenty-Year Marriage   24
Whatever Monster   25
Divorce, an Elegy   26

TWO

Weather Report   29
How Gravity Hated Us   30
Dilaudid   31
After the Search Party   32
Easy Poem for My Sister   33
For the Man Waiting By the Monkey Bars   34
Falling in Love with Flash Gordon   35
I Have Always Loved to Skip   36
Lexicons   37
Yearbook Photo of My Parents, 1959   38
Ford Galaxie 500   39
The Caller   40
Rustic Poem for My Mother   41
Stories I Know   42

THREE

Nocturne and Dream Song   45

At the Speed of Light   46

Watching the Late-Late Movie: Imagining
      My Ex-Wife as Buck Rogers' Love Interest   47

We're Always Getting the Story Wrong   48

Plan 9 Sonnenizio from Outer Space   49

My Love is for the Weatherman   50

What I Did to Make You Love Me   51

For the Girl Who Cast Spells with Food   52

Robert Oppenheimer's Thesis   53

Reading the Student's Evaluation   54

Post-Dated Love Note on the Doomsday Planetary
      Alignment: 5 May 2000   55

Letter from a Mistress   56

Love Note Sent Over a Long Distance   57

The Balloon   58

She Dreams of the Stork   60

If Pain Weren't Already Your Husband   61

Brief Notes on Helio-Galactic Lullabies   63

Collect Call   65

Acknowledgments   71

About the Author   78

ONE

Based on a True Story

                    Inspired by actual events
are the blueberries, the bird

I folded into origami and willed
            to fly

Also true:
I've spun the light and made a magic show
of the planets

                    while stars collapsed
through the atmosphere

They threw their light between us

as I made a wish for you
                    to love me and you did

not   My calendar's circled with dates
                    where my lips and heart have simultaneously moved

but said different things

And now I have worked an iron lung into a song about love

The flowers on the sill still lean toward sunlight
            when you walk by

rocking your hips all through Arkansas
            ringing phones
just so you can say goodbye

Watching an Esther Williams Film After My Wife's Affair

In this film, there's a metaphor: love
as the intercostal waterways, and somewhere
Esther has jackknifed from the plank of a pirate ship

and surfaced wearing only
her favorite bathing suit. It's a sequence
in a dream because the plot doesn't need

any more danger. She's doing underwater aerobics
and swimmy kicks like a skinny Shelley Winters
in that film about escape where everybody dies.

It's my kind of flick—the type critics
line up to love after the fact. Eventually a villain must come
in. A white whale killer. Some badass

of aquatic mischief I can't predict. Maybe
they'll race a cigarette boat halfway to Haiti
or marry along the underwater line of the equator.

Whatever happens, it must've been hard
to keep the boom mike out of the frame
and get this down on film.

Or maybe it was all just *lights,*
camera, action, some serious splish-splash,
the director telling Esther to paddle deeper in.

The Crossing

Under winter's deck of stars,
my neighbor advances onto the pond, careful
as ever, each step a test
of the uneasy ice.

On the bank behind him, his wife.
Before him, the lover he cannot get over.

All winter I've watched his nightly back-and-forth.
But tonight my wife pulls the curtains closed.

She shuts off the lamp, tumbles
her braid down her back.

Her true love stands in the shut dark
of her eyes—waiting
beneath the thinnest strip of moon.

In our bed, there's only
a sudden collapse of ice.

Sterile

My wife can't stop hurting when she sees children.
They coil in her dreams, knees raised
to their stomachs, feet stamping their rhythms.

She's reminded of high school, how she pulled up
her dress in loneliness and a man laughed at her.
But never mind that. I have my gun

collection out. I can't stop pointing and clicking
the trigger at the open window. But the birds
won't die. They flutter away, startled by the swing

of my aim. They land on the fence
of the city swimming pool. There the children run
off the diving board, ducking invisible bullets.

To the Double Helix

I've climbed up to the attic to stare
into the crib I've taken up here, its emptiness
no different than the womb that waits for me

downstairs. I can't conceive of a higher power, so I pray
to you, Double Helix of Our Children Unraveling
in the Womb, Our Saint of Apoptosis. Look

at the candles I've arranged and lit, the diet
I've given myself over to, the miles I run
in bargain for your favor. You, from whom

all paternity proceeds, it's on nights like these
I try to hide, creep farther across the beams
whenever she calls for me. God,

how I fear the grisly machinery inside of her—
blood in the spokes, miswelded DNA, another
month of trying.   But Sir, she's waiting

and I have to go. Please fill her basket
with your whisper, your perfect winding ladder.
There must be rust inside of her

to account for all this dying.

Stork

Tonight I am looking for you.
In the market, several women confess

they have seen you defenseless
against the children there. They tear

fistfuls of your feathers as you limp,
nearly bald, back into flight.

Tonight I am looking for you
to reclaim your fine down, to break

the windows of sleeping men
hoarding your plumes in their pillows.

Your ghost is circling the city. I am
looking for you like an expectant falconer,

my arm raised against the sky.

Ultrasound

We've come to see it—
the slumbering world
in the airless bowl

of the amnion.
Conjured by the monitor,
its heart thrums

a silver rhythm—
tiny pulses we count
in the black hole

of its chest.
Impressive, this orb,
its gravitational pull

on us. So small, still
something convinces:
it's the most important

planet. We watch it
ripple through its atmosphere
of slowly rolling stars.

Around this sleeping
sphere we orbit:
impatient astronauts.

Wolf

Caused by a deletion of chromosome 4, Ulrich Wolf Syndrome produces death in the bulk of children born with it.

—*rarediseases.com*

I've sweated through the panting night.

I prowl the hills above the house
where you've hidden our daughter
from the fangs

of my DNA, the chemistry
firing this bloodstream.

Black satellites signal me
to skulk the pasture with the soft paw
of the body, to snap the hasp
and climb inside the kitchen window.

A wolf's no scavenger.
Hunger licks its tongue
across the danger of my teeth.

I snuffle after our daughter's scent
rising like a light below a door
in a darkened hallway.

I've sharpened my claws on the black night
of the kitchen. The moon's burning out
in the bottom of my bowl.

Our daughter's so little,
I could swallow her whole.

There Was No Funeral

because death doesn't stagger, it walks
on arched toes, hangs sheets
over mirrors,

because soon the house will fill with no one
who saw you lift your skirt and wade
into the ether,

because I will undress the bed, thread
by thread,

because I still have business
in this world.

Mexico's Waters Are Only for Newlyweds

No one welcomes our bodies in Puerto Vallarta.
They fear we witch its waters with marital failure.

An affair every even year of marriage and this is another
makeshift reconciliation—mojitos and a week of beach

we've charged to our credit card: penance
of the easiest order. Each morning, your footprints lead

from the beach to me where you love my body
against the grit we've shaken off in sleep. Sand everywhere,

we've given up on trying to stay clean. Twenty years of marriage—
my lust's no longer monstrous, your sarong has little left

to hide. The wave-wet sand won't welcome us
the way it did the night you took my family's name.

The sky was honey-mooned that night, its light golden
across your shoulders. Today is only sun-blast in our eyes

as we stare beachward toward the newlyweds
who shimmer like the wished-on dimes I've wasted in the hotel fountain.

The Last Known Love Letter of Poseidon

My seabed brings no sleep without you near.
Insomnia's all that travels these darksome waters.
Our headboard slapped for years like feeble shutters
storm-torn by hurricanes our bodies raised.

But now I hear your elbows dimple sands
beyond my salty grip. You're unimpressed
by ships I've twisted into sticks and tossed
toward the beaches drinking up my seas.

My power can pull down any stubborn star
my finger chooses but cannot draw you back.
I wonder at the clatter coming from the dock:
Is someone knocking my name from off your boat?

Els Van Doren fell 13,000 feet to her death after her parachute and emergency parachute both failed to open. A fellow female skydiver is suspected of tampering with the chutes after learning Van Doren was having an affair with her boyfriend.

Using the Earth as a Blunt-Force Object

takes no aim or timing. The physics
are unconscionable yet simple: the object
of your beloved's wayward affections
freefalls at 9.8 meters per second squared, the rate
at which gravity becomes the greatest
accomplice.
　　　　　The sky is full
of surprises, and down here,
we're constantly watching. These days
something is always falling—
meteors and probes, the occasional
lover.
　　　　　Each week, Professor Science
makes it clear on TV: Hell hath no fury
like the Earth. Consider the orbs
it has scorned and pulled into the burning
clutch of its atmosphere.
　　　　　　　　　Before burnout,
they too plunged, convinced
the air was enough to catch them.

All My Grudges I've Given Your Name

How little shame I have, considering the many pities
of our feud.
        For instance, the sympathetic stress
of our myna bird, the one that learned to replicate

my voice.
        Morning after morning
we saw its cage sagged with the weight of feathers
it had plucked and spat about itself. The morning

        we found it dead beneath its perch, I knew
there was no one left to hear my pleas

for harmony. That you had given it my name—that black
        irony—was inescapable. So

all my grudges I've given your name,
        which means *noble*, which means *truth*.

My left and bony hand coming back tonight, clawing deep
        in the dirt where you laid that bird to rest . . . well,

how you'll tremble in the morning

when you see it at the end
        of my boot trail, its hollow body positioned just so
beneath the smeary prints
        I've left on your window.

Twenty-Year Marriage

Beside me in bed her arm
crosses the arch of her nose,
and I think: Radishes,
she is the color of radishes.

Once we hovered above our bed.
A kiss like a paper cut
brought us back.

Now, she slips from sleep
and ties herself to balloons.

Her weight is unimaginable.

I lean out the window and watch
the red dots climb
and finally disappear.

Whatever Monster

I'm sad for what our bodies never made,
for the days we rose, fully rested, from sleep
no childish thing had interrupted. What's made
our lives a stalled biology doesn't sleep;
it clamors in the womb, scaring children.
Our nightstand spills with useless cures we've tried.
Whatever monster turns our would-be children
to blood each month cannot be stopped (we've tried).

On lusty nights let's cinch ourselves together,
knowing the halves we have to put together
won't come to something we can love together.
And when we feel alone, let's face each other
and do the things we could only do together,
like say we're happy to convince each other.

Divorce, an Elegy

That night the sky shivered and she floated
to the moon. From below I watched
her liftoff—the whole neighborhood,
one by one, opening doors and peering up
and up from the shrinking mounds
of our lives. For weeks I arched my feet and waited

for gravity to grow itself into a myth.
But I never left the Earth, wheeling
my way to weightlessness. Each night
I blasted *Ground control to Major Tom.*
She pantomimed a woman straining to understand
but I knew she heard everything
over the buzzing telegraph of stars.

The neighbors borrowed her tools, stuffed
their closets with clothes she couldn't wear;
someone took over for her at the school. Eventually,
we found we didn't even speak
of her, except at night, when floating
in our pools, when we saw the moon
beam her body all over Arkansas.

TWO

Weather Report

Tonight the weather report says tornadoes
won't throw our homes moonward.
But I keep driving. Two blocks over

I hear the train they say comes
only to rip up real estate. If at home,
I'd open a window, lie

in the tub, hold onto myself.   Here, I have nothing
to keep me from spinning
two miles south. Once my sister

did pirouettes through the city park
saying, *I'm a leaf blown by a twister.*
Four years later, she boarded a train

with a man who turned her head
six times against the edge of a knife.
That day was supposed to be sunny

but rain came for eight days straight.
Tonight, too, the forecast is wrong.
Tornadoes are swinging homes

from the swirled horizon, unstaking fences
that keep the earth pinned,
and mark the road I'm driving.

How Gravity Hated Us

My sister was the first to learn how gravity hated
our family—a spinning plunge into the gorge

of echoy quartz when she failed to cling
to air like Father imagined. Her hollow bones

made him certain she'd been born
for flight so he'd splayed her among the tools of his shop

and stripped the rivets from her body,
took her inside his shower and shaved her

nose into a beak. Her talons scratched
for balance as she crept across her perch,

eyes rolling over the canyons as she stumbled
into free-fall and Earth climbed up to meet her.

She rose, coughing teeth into her palms,
shivering impact-rubble from her shoulders,

trembling in the feathery shadow of our father
whose fingers were already fitting me with wings.

Dilaudid

Sweet devil of my mouth, you strike me like slow lightning,
drag ravaged twilight behind my eyes. Sugar cube,

crepuscular angel, O my filthy licorice: uncorked,
you're the fiddle music of my youth, the cure

I took for broken bones when, dared, I scaled
the church steeple and fell. Laudanum,

the doctor said, lowering the spoon. After that,
my thumb was always under my hammer's aim. Cuts, bruises—

everything craved your tinctured kiss: Mother's long finger
dipped in the yoke of the bottle, touched to my expectant tongue.

After the Search Party

Something silent must've passed
between the boy and girl,
between lunch and recess,

that lured them into the woods to watch
each other undress. The teachers lined us up
and touched our heads, ensuring

our presence, that our adolescence hadn't followed
that scent into the trees, that our innocence
could still be accounted for.

How I'd wanted to be the one
to find them, to be the one who understood.
But all that was left

was to stare as their parents approached
from their cars. It was their embarrassment
that finally made me look away. The detached way

they looked at their kids, as though
they could read their children's actions
in our eyes, could see them naked

for the very first time.

Easy Poem for My Sister

—after Stephen Orlen

Mothers had their names for girls like her.
Fifteen and already the town pump, she'd lie
in bed and count the boys, their faces

like beads on a rosary of ruin. Her whoredom—
old news by high school. By 20,
the name of an unlucky town

men were always passing through. Trollop,
tramp. The Sisters of the Good Shepherd
tried to save her. But I knew

they could never make her
into a Mary Magdalene—a whore
that even Catholics could love. College.

Law school. She left her panties on
the floors of her professors' homes. She walked
like she didn't owe herself a thing, a law

of diminishing returns. She hated
her clothes so she took them off. Jezebel. Strumpet.
Father had his names for girls like her.

For the Man Waiting by the Monkey Bars

Thirteen was never easy for a boy whose mother
never wanted him home. So I let you.

And afterward, you lit us cigarettes and let the latest
AM hits sing from their black bed of scratches.

I wondered if this was how all grownups did it—dizzy
with nicotine and Top 40 circling on the stereo.

Still unzipped, you said you had to show me how
your Ouija board worked—fat fingers sliding

over letters that spelled something horrible
if I ever told.   For weeks I climbed over signs

that warned to keep out after dark. I walked slow
through parking lots, waited by the monkey bars

for your return. In the nights that flickered
in front of the television, I wondered if you ever touched

your room's brown paneling and thought of my hair.
Did you see a star's slow fall and miss me at all?

When police tugged you ducking through their lights,
was I the only name on your lips? Tell me

you were listening to those records to remember how
the sweet tremble in my voice brushed against your ear.

Falling in Love with Flash Gordon

Of all of us falling in love
         with Flash Gordon & Dale Arden

in the theater that night, could any others have known
                  the soundtrack masked the sounds of two boys

& their first tentative kisses?   No,
                  not until the usher's sudden flashlight
         exposed us for what we were.

Faggots, he said
                  as he dragged
         our mothers' numbers around the rotary dial.

How my mother could've known
                  what the usher named me or why
         she repeated it when our car doors closed

I couldn't say.   Nor explain how the name
                  found me the following Monday at school.

         But once it did, all the love notes
I dropped in his locker went unanswered
         except one

that read: Your love is like a slow-motion death ray
from outer space,
                  like the one Flash stopped
just seconds before Earth would've been scattered into atoms.

I Have Always Loved to Skip

I did so to the field where the flyer
crashed into the silo, spilling
oats everywhere in the wilderness
below. Blood drenched the limbs
of the pilot, whose eyes were still
alive, rolling side to side
over his mouth, his tongue, raspberry
to a point, pleading with itself
to say something about getting up
for help. I stepped over the rope
of weeds between us, careful
not touch him though it seemed
he needed it. His fingers clawed
at what I can only imagine
he thought were crows coming
to peck among the oats.
My father said he'd seen something
like it in the war, that clawing.
But mother wouldn't hear of it
at the table. She carried our plates
to the porch. Families had gathered
at the steps. They wanted to know
what I'd seen, to hear me tell it slow,
not to skip a thing.

Lexicons

On the steamer Mother learned the only words
she needed to know:

Yes. More.

She pressed her tongue to their shapes,
held their sounds like cigarette smoke.

On Ellis Island, she learned *Please*
was a worthless word. Throw it away
like an old love letter. Answer their questions
softly:

Are you well? *Yes.*
Why did you come? *More.*

She pushed her cheek to the cool squares
of the kitchen's black and white floor.

In the building's basement, boys found her
folding laundry, their tongues wet
with America, their hands full

of its money. Down the street, she touched the glass
of the candy case. The boys' sweeping hands

meant *choose.* At home, she unfolded the chocolate
from its foil. From outside the boys called.
Her mother stood up but meant *Close the window.*

Yearbook Photo of My Parents, 1959

In the picture, Mother's not my mother yet.
Lithe and barely 20, she leans into the frame

of the sorority kissing booth, eager
to meet his lips.

He's counted out his love, professed it
dime by dime.

They've kissed like this for 60 years
inside the camera-snap,

their ardor unchanged by time.
But the camera's caught more than that:

my father's restraint.
Barely there in the flash

of history, his face inches
forward from the photo's lower corner, watching

the footballer whose kiss shuts my mother's eyes
like rapture.

In the picture, it's nearly 1960.
My parents' faces young, unworried

with the future. Soon they'd graduate
to a life they never imagined, not knowing

how often this kiss would be remembered
every time my father wanted to fight.

Ford Galaxie 500

Through the back windshield
the world looks
like any other small town. This 1959 fin-fixed
space ship is blasting

the radio. The last transmission came
from Little Rock. *Darling, I know you send me.*
Mother, I have a problem.

Try to hold it.
There's a milk jug if you can't.

The motel is the moon
parked on the back of a parking lot. The astronaut we've come to meet
is not my father.

In Texas, the waitress called me
Cutie Pie and put down two creamers and a spoon
she shined on her thigh. The astronaut counted down
5-4-3-2-1 the bites I had left
of my hot fudgey. Last time he gave me

a half-pack of Wrigley's. I chewed until they came
out of the room, my mother's face red as an apple, his smile
like one on TV.

We're lifting off from the last part of the highway.
We're heading for home. Father's filing saws
for wood they'll never use on the moon.

The Caller

It was late. The man
was a mumble on the other end
of the receiver. Something

you'd say to a lover, I heard
my father accuse my mother.

Night after night, my father
put his ear to the wire
that cut a wound inside of him.

He'd re-cradle the receiver and I'd fall
asleep to the grunt
of my parents' mattress.

Mother was the first to the phone
when the calls started in the afternoon.
Solicitations, credit card come-ons, never

something you'd say to a lover. At night,
she'd smoke beside my father
until the TV turned blue.

But when she thought he wouldn't notice,
she'd stare at where her thoughts
had gone, at what was

and wasn't there
in the silence of the telephone.

Rustic Poem for My Mother

Buckeye and birch, your body
was a glow of hardwood trees
no logger could resist. The worst
sawed the night with bunkhouse dreams

of walking your perimeter
and carving terror in the beauty
of your interior. He courted the elm
and oak of your desire, swore

he loved you before the polished
mahogany of a church. Walnut
and alder, sweet gum and spruce,
he felled you on your wedding night

with a honeymoon of skidders.
Years later, you looked at him
like scrub pine, drove away, leaving him
like cordwood you'd cut and piled for somebody else.

Stories I Know

Father, I've driven to the drive-in of your past and parked beneath the
clapboard screen to imagine the stories I know. It's here that you proposed
to Mother when the screen stars kissed in the foreground of a B-movie
mushroom cloud. Is this the scene you see in your anesthetized sleep?
You won't find Mother there among the overgrown weeds, the gutted
refreshment stand. No alchemy of memory can unmake her grave.

When your friends gathered, they told of the night the projection booth
snapped and ghosted Hepburn onto her coat.

But Father, don't rock back in time. Mother won't glimmer down to meet
you. She was willowy and young, but dead now so long, how would you
Even know her—this woman you once said you loved.

THREE

Nocturne and Dream Song

That first year I hardly slept, going each night
to swim in the lake's bowl of stars, listening to

the paddle of my palms as I struggled toward the middle.
I wanted to hear the voices of children drowned there

in the wet undergrowth of memory, to find the girl
whose song was so simple, that when I listened,

I'd know how joy was possible.
Instead I saw my daughter, a ghost on the surface, her eyes

flashlight beams scaring away the darkness.
My own eyes rested over the rim of the water

as she went past, her arms rowing the quiet
out of the water. Each morning

I'd wake in the drench of my bed sheets, still feeling
the tiny wet hands that had tucked me in.

At the Speed of Light

Professor Science made certain everyone knew the danger
of two bodies missing the mark in matrimony: kids
roll off the cosmos when satellites don't move in sync.

But all couples experience technical difficulties.
Audiences laughed when Jackie Gleason wanted Alice
on the moon—his bus driver's cap knocked back,

his belly bigger than any planet. At home,
something was always going wrong at mission control.
Mother scrawling love notes. Father tearing them up.

It's a wonder they ever landed on the moon.

Tonight I snap the TV off and watch it swallow
all the sitcom's light. Somewhere my wife's
a cruising photon emission. She says she's coming

back fast as the speed of light. But some things travel
faster than the speed of light and light doesn't always
travel very fast.

Watching the Late-Late Movie: Imagining My Ex-Wife as Buck Rogers' Love Interest

Fighting the Martian hordes, you were the most,
Miss Deering: rocking zero-gravity
peep-toes and skirts, averting tragedy
with Buck each week in grainy kinescope.

You kicked it fresh in the television future,
distracting Killer Kane and his horny minions,
your atomic push-up bra and death-ray nylons
the bait that Buck could use to cinch their capture.

But Wilma, this is how I would've had it.
We would've chilled right here on Earth, got floaty
on gin and chase and cans of Douggen-Dirby.
The doom-prone world we'd leave for Buck alone.
We'd jitterbug until the stars were done,
sticking to Earth like gravity was a habit.

We're Always Getting the Story Wrong

The film tells of a gigantic, island-dwelling ape named Kong who dies in an attempt to possess a woman.

They're out there flying, those tiny machines,
the wind-up birds that want to carry my love
from the cradle of my hand. I hear them rushing

in the shiny distance, see them buzzing
black rings around my head, trying to calm
the shrieks of their metal wings by diving down at me.

I think how my thumb swipes across her body
and something thumps inside her chest, how
if those machines would let me, I'd pour oil

along the noise of their necks and clear
the caked ore from the engine of their jaws. Instead,
I hear the sound of their biplane wings shearing off.

How I marvel at their speed as they ping past, my hands wanting
but so useless to hold them.

Plan 9 Sonnenizio from Outer Space

If I should learn, in some quite casual way,
that horrors roared their way from outer space
to paralyze the living sum of Earth
and somehow resurrect the resting dead

and I, as Chief of Saucer Operations,
had learned the ghouls I'd seen atop some graveyard
plots were part of fuzzy plans to keep
some doomsday scheme from going off—

you best believe you'd find me acting casual.
I'd call and chit-chat this and chit-chat that.
Eventually you'd learn we were the world's
sole occupants and strut your stuff my way.

Like primitive props someone strung from above,
we'd wobble like a saucer when we made love.

My Love is for the Weatherman

My love is for the weatherman, his secret
code of cumulus. Nights, revved up,
I call him up at the darkened studio

of my mind, his body bent over
a radar aimed at tomorrow. I'm on my knees each time
the humidity reaches a hundred, my blood

a barometer and all the needles spinning.
On the couch, playful kisses, we make
love through a high pressure system, my breasts

mismatched clouds over the field of his body.
My family wonders at the attraction but I've fallen
for his assurances—that I'll be here

to witness what the weather changes. Each night
I'm waiting when he turns on destiny,
ready to hear what rain can't even know.

What I Did to Make You Love Me

I wiggled my nose just like a TV witch
each time you went away, brewed thick elixirs
with bottles of discount liquor—smoky potions
to end your resistance to my lovesick wishes.
I recited phrases from my favorite spell-maker,
ad-libbed some lines from songs I knew you loved.
My old Black Sabbath records got played backwards
in spinning rituals of makeshift suburban magic.

But my abracadabras made nothing happen.
I emptied out the last of my worthless potions,
gathered my records back inside their jackets.
I'm certain you were sleeping in the middle
of this bewitching—indifferent succubus,
hugging your hands to your uncharmable heart.

For the Girl Who Cast Spells with Food

You were nothing like those three in the forest—
the sisters whose beauty came to ruin
in the rising steam of their forest cauldron.
Each night you laid your spells before us,

a sprig of mint for garnish; parsley,
your scattered familiar. Night by night
we lived in a flourish of eating, caught
in the ritual of it. How you charmed me

was the easiest bewitchery:
your *côte de veau*, your *pâte à choux*.
For you, the food was more than sex,
for me, the doubling of a mystery.

But that was how I wanted your secrets—
with magic, with lust, with entremets.

Robert Oppenheimer's Thesis

must have been genius. But I like
to think of him before all that:
his Harvard reading room, the dog-eared pages
of everything—*Popular Mechanics,*
Poetry, Scientific American, maybe
Monarch Notes for whatever
wasn't available. In the corner,
a space robot with killer pinchers,
a soft disposition and a heart
that pumped Plutonium-239.

Night and day, Bob lumbering
through his room of radioactive dust,
his black-rimmed glasses blurred
by atomic fallout, his eyes spiraling
like a B-movie hypnotism screen—
that's Oppenheimer to me. Bob
in the quad. Bob out for coffee.
Bob shot down by girls in a bar.
The *real* Robert Oppenheimer. Before
he made the world an atom bomb,
when he just wanted some machine
to cough a pickup line to him.

Reading the Student's Evaluation

You've lectured all semester: *Love's the single subject*
resistant to physics. But F=MA, where F
is force and M is me attracted.

I'd like to simulate the impulse of an engine
exceeding its mass, the only motion principle
I remember. Jet propulsion

is simple and the moon is very near.
To fly me there, apply
forward propulsive thrust. Or rear.

Post-Dated Love Note on the Doomsday Planetary Alignment: 5 May 2000

"With all of the planets aligned on one side of the solar system, astrophysicists feared the gravitational pull would snap Earth's axis and send the planet careening into outer space."
                                        —Dr. Hans Craig, NASA

When they claimed it'd be like Earth had never been—
us catapulted across the blinking map
of satellites, spun down in a noose of doom—

I wanted only you to barrel-roll
with me across the blazy swirl of stars.
And if it'd been like Earth had never been,

we'd lost our grip on gravity together,
gone ass-over-elbow when things went tilt.
The satellites spun. Down came the news of doom

and I imagined us as just another
set of heavenly bodies spooning through
the universe. The Earth had never been

so useless as it would've been right then—
us hovering in lusty weightlessness
while satellites spun down their news of doom.

When they claimed it'd be like Earth had never been
and satellites spun down their news of doom,
we would've been the greatest constellations
to ever swing from lines of glittered starshine.

Letter from a Mistress

I was a bird when you wanted a wife.
So I flew, collecting what I knew of wives—
hotel keys to unlock
the lace they lay across their down-
less bodies, champagne
corks to keep their mouths
from buzzing all the flowers.

You made me a hummingbird. Blur
of desire. A word, sir. Finish
what you started. Here is where
you hung your promises. Hear them
hiss across my body.

Love Note Sent Over a Long Distance

—after Stokesbury

Women fake it across my screen
        but fail to help me in my endeavor
                to love myself. Divided

from you in this lonely state
        of Arkansas, I've laid hands
                only on myself, prayed

for communion. Between Fayetteville
        and where you are, the map's dark
                dot is Mena. All roads are clear

so I must ask that you kindly avail yourself
        of me in that dim locale and soon.
                There exists a definite need!

There on rented sheets we'll meet
        in the middle of our bodies, ignore
                the bedside Gideon. A fruitless

        Adam and Eve, let's improvise.

The Balloon

—after Saba

It came like joy—
untethered, sudden.

An escaped toy
from a nearby garden,
a mishandled prop
in a magic show—.

It cleared the row
of finance houses
but climbed no farther,

as if my gaze
from inside the diner
had stayed its orbit.

So plain in its blueness,
I might've missed it.

But how it charmed me.

I left my plate
and watched from under
the sky. The streets
had ceased their thunder.

In that quiet—crying.
I saw the boy, his reaching
for what he'd lost.

Whatever spell
had been, was broken
in that call.

She Dreams of the Stork

—for Johnathon

It flew into the cavern
of her body and hovered
the fertile waters, spent
months perched
on the post of her garden.

Each time it flexed its way
into flight, its talons knived
the water and split branches
the length of the empty cradle
to shoo the gathering crows.

She says she has felt
its feathery blur at night, found
strange plumage in a spray
upon her pillows. She can't know
when she repeats these things

the times I've found her framed
in these farmhouse windows,
spooling herself into a circle
to mimic the rounds
of a natural nest. At dusk

she calls me to witness
her white inventions, has me
touch the warmth her hands
have spread across the bed
of imaginary hatchlings.
Her voice is a careful treble

when she leans to explain
the eggs' soft hues.
I'll trample through the chill
one evening and hug these

wishful visions from her, cup
the swell of her stomach, the bird
winging beneath my touch.

If Pain Weren't Already Your Husband

If pain weren't already your husband,
I would gladly be. We'd hold hands and smile
in ambulance rides, our faces bathed
beneath the red wail and splash
of rescue lights.

Our hospital bed would move by electric power.
Breathless and connected
to switches, we'd need oxygen
when we'd made love right.

And when you went down
under the knife, I'd travel that rope
of anesthesia with you. Sympathetic
surgery. Identical sutures.

We'd laugh in post-op about the altar,
how wrecked by lust, we'd rushed the priest
through his litany of vows. With this pain,
I thee wed. I do, I do, I do.

Drunk on punch, we'd wobble to the limo.
You knew when the honeymoon was over,
I'd carry you across the threshold.

Brief Notes on Helio-Galactic Lullabies

Song after song, it's become obvious

the sun is not the lone alto
astronomers once believed

but a chorus of atoms breaking
into lullabies.
Out there our planets

have been lulled and are falling fast
asleep. Even our most confident

astronauts aren't certain of what to expect
should Earth fail to open

its eyes in time to catch them
at splashdown.

But little has changed on Earth
for us. You still keep to your orbit,
sending your wishes

to disinterested stars. Should you find
in your slumber that you're among those

celestial bodies, sleepwalking—
that suddenly you're wombed

with a child so round
that it startles you from sleep—

call me. I'll transmit to you
a lullaby like Earth

has never heard.

Collect Call

Somewhere out there, an operator plugged in
       the wire of your voice to the switchboard

of Arkansas where I am
       happy to accept the charges—an act so antique
          I think of *Sputnik* beeping

overhead, lovers petting in Buicks
       and glowing with the green of radium dials.

But what you've called to say is lost
       in the line's wreckage of crackle and static.

The night you went away
       the interstate glowed red beneath the flaring
          fins of your father's Cadillac.

Now this collect call
       from outer space & what you've called to say
          is clear at last: Among stars

lovers come and go easy as you please. It's the gravity
       of Earth that makes letting go so hard.

Acknowledgments

Grateful acknowledgement to the following publications in which these poems first appeared (sometimes in a different form or under a different title):

32 Poems
"My Love is for the Weatherman"

Barn Owl Review
"Watching an Esther Williams Film after My Wife's Affair"

Blackbird
"All My Grudges I've Given Your Name"

Black Warrior Review
"Using the Earth as Blunt-Force Object"

Crab Orchard Review
"Falling in Love with Flash Gordon"

Cream City Review
"Whatever Monster"

DIAGRAM
"Robert Oppenheimer's Thesis"

Diner
"Stork"

diode
"There Was No Funeral," "Dilaudid," "For the Man by the Monkey Bars,"
    "We're Always Getting the Story Wrong," "To the Double Helix"

Kenyon Review Online
"Wolf"

Lo.Ball
"Watching the Late-Late Movie," "The Last Known Love Letter of Poseidon,"
    "Easy Poem for My Sister"

Measure
"What I Did to Make You Love Me"

Melic Review
"Twenty-Year Marriage"

New England Review
"Collect Call," "Based on a True Story"

Nimrod
"Mexico's Waters are Only for Newlyweds"

Open Windows
"Divorce, An Elegy"

PebbleLakeReview
"Post-Dated Love Note on the Doomsday Planetary Alignment," "Brief Notes on Helio-Galactic Lullabies," "Ultrasound," "Letter from a Mistress"

The Pedestal
"Weather Report"

Quarterly West
"Rustic Poem for My Mother," "If Pain Weren't Already Your Husband"

Rattle
"Sterile"

Stickman Review
"Through the Back Windshield," "I Have Always Loved to Skip"

"Through the Back Windshield" was reprinted in the *Rhysling Anthology of Best Science Fiction, Fantasy and Horror Poetry* (2005).

"Lexicons" appeared in *A Face to Meet the Faces: An Anthology of Contemporary Persona Poetry.*

"How Gravity Hated Us" appeared in *Best New Poets 2011.*

"Letter from a Mistress" and "Yearbook Photo of My Parents, 1959" were reprinted in *The Gulf Stream: Poems from the Gulf Coast.*

I am grateful to Johnathon Williams, Jon Cool, Velvet Hall Cool, and Kurt and Susan Andrews whose friendship has been invaluable to me. This book would not have been completed without the help of my first readers and teachers, Corey Marks, Davis McCombs, Geoffrey Brock, Michael Heffernan, Bruce Bond, William Ryan, Jack Heflin, and Anthony Farrington. Thanks also to D.A. Powell, Sandy Longhorn, Anthony Robinson, Hannah Craig, Steve Mueske, and members of various poetry workshops, particularly at the University of Arkansas, who read and commented with considerable attention and care. My unspeakable gratitude goes to J.P. Dancing Bear and Dream Horse Press who believed in this book when I failed to do so. Finally, I'm immensely indebted to Kathleen Bowen—my world, my light, my partner on this fool's walk—whose strength has carried me through.

In Memoriam, Shirl Brunell (1934—2006)

About the Author

Ash Bowen holds an MFA and PhD in creative writing. He lives with his partner and step-children in Alabama, where he teaches creative writing and literature at the U of A in Tuscaloosa.

www.ingramcontent.com/pod-product-compliance
Lightning Source LLC
Chambersburg PA
CBHW021511090426
42739CB00007B/563